cradle a

cradle ages

cradle ages

cradle ages

cradle ages

cradle ages

part one

dedicated to those moments that one never forgets but
almost always change you

my mind ages before my body does
too many hardships that my young bones can't hold
too many lessons that my youthful face can't capture

generational trauma
everything and everyone has a narrative
point of views may vary
but roll the tape
because some things can't be denied
some things are just as they are
tallies for every time my presence grew an invisibility cloak
marks for every brutal lash they covered
scars for every cruel word they swept under the rug

angry adults
bullies are made
when we were younger,
we would fight
they would separate us in the night
reprimanded to stop the fighting
but you were the one instigating
bullies take flight
and if only someone held you accountable
stopped you in your childish ways
if only someone told you that wasn't okay
instead,
you shushed me
invalidated the lies
and handed out scotch-free passes
to this day,
it's still the same
ignored and forgotten
we were both quiet
but only one of us silenced
only one of us speaking volumes

one-sided

talk to me like an empty wall
bounce off your ideas, thoughts, and beliefs
because i'm happy if you're happy
so tell me what you need
i will nod and listen
for i love you so

a people pleaser is born
ignore me so my innocent conscience grows guilty
brood so my empathic soul abandons her post of dignity
twist my reality so i believe i am wrong
muddle my words so that my language isn't my own
hurt me with your passive silence
weaponize my self-depreciation
make my identity an extension of yours
i shall only want what you want
like what you like
see what you see
think what you think
believe what you believe
i am better this way to you
i die
a people pleaser born

narcissism
wanting to feel needed
always an audience to your one man show
string me along
keep me on my toes
chasing at your heels
play with my anxiety
wavering in my nerves
snap at me
make me feel guilty
the center of attention is your home
the cycle of abuse is your local road
like a looped track field,
you walk it on repeat
play unfair
deny second place at all costs
don't mean what you say
attention, admiration, repeat
rob others of the peace they build
empire of ego made from stolen building blocks
projecting guilt on the innocent
obligating the reserved
feeling needed for the wrong reasons
and like a self-built matrix
adored for a false perception

abused
actions don't mean that much to me anymore
your words have done enough
there is enough levity without the weight of action
behind them
i'd like to consider myself a rather forgiving person
i know i am no saint
but the past is very rough for us
and trust cannot live between us
i won't be a victim of you
i will not succumb to a stale life
filled with a constant rendition of your emasculation,
domination, and humiliation
if i must be a victim,
i will be my own
for i am still not the same
we collided
i broke
and you left the scene of the crime

abyss
did i jump or did you push me?
i know you didn't go with me for i am all alone
i am a broken leg with no crutch to lean
falling, falling, falling deep into my own thoughts
sunken hole so deep in my chest there's no room for my
lungs to breathe
who am i?
you tell me
i'll believe you more
who I am?
i might never fully know
are you happy that i'm here?
if you could send me a life raft,
would you?
guilty conscience sports an innocent pride,
while my anxious heart hosts a lost soul

today
everything i managed to keep blocked out of my mind
catapulted out of my mouth
like a shaken soda bottle
i was always bound to implode

unfortunate reminiscing
to have symmetry,
it should be assumed that something is consistent and can
guarantee success
i only want symmetry in my life
i want what i see to be a perfect, inimitable reflection of
your own
i don't want obstinance

why do they tell you when you're young how awful it is
to grow?
can i not change any faster?
my youth is slow and stagnant
my growing pains awkward and stiff
why make me hate this season of life when i can't change
the weather of the storm?

you may never go back to my ripe young age
but my experience remains unstained
i sit in your hatred for this season of striping pinnacles
i was happier with my ignorance
i don't need to know that life gets better than this
i'd rather be surprised than forced to sit in futile patience

life may get better
yet still,
it won't pass me by any sooner
and I am wiser than to wish it away faster

a part of you
you are a part of me
but i am not the same to you
context is everything when it comes to us
you are my everything
i am your ease
you are my priority
i am your obligation
you are my reason
I am your reminder
context is everything when it comes to us
it is where I lay the foundation of my excuses
it is where I lose my reasoning and find my lies
ignorant fool that cheats themselves of truth
my life lacks
for i would rather be the second version of you
if others only knew the contents of my life,
they would stop asking the context of my unhappiness

cradle ages

monopolistic aura
crowded aroma
chaos erupted
rattled throat
and rocky stomachs
- **what you do to me**

tell me
let's skip the fight
just tell me you hate me
tell me to go
tell me all the things i do to you
tell me i'm a child
tell me i'm useless
now expect me to act like an adult
tell me i'm good,
 but only when
tell me you love me,
 but only if
let me internalize your words
let me perfect myself
let me always believe I could do better
let me live through stress, doubt, and worry
now tell me you hate to see me like this

"i'm tired of this"
said the little girl to the older
tough exterior and hollow inside
little girl that never grew with her outer shell
instead,
she roams and stretches within her newfound space
lost within the maze she fades
"i'm tired of this"
said the little girl to the older version
tired love and secondhand hours
"me too"
said the older to the little
but our growth was stunted
our appetite small
we can't handle real futures with our tiny child belly
all we have are the scrapes we've learned to slowly chew

history books
why do adults misbehave?
young and lacking in trips around the sun
yet I can still sense this course of action should only ignite
a deep fire of implausible guilt

a strong calling to do different
a fiery anxiousness to change
but you don't

and still,
you must know best
that is the narrative we tell our children
and our children's children
and our children's children
until enough generations pass and history meets culture
conscious meets evolution
it's then that we can admit defeat
and acknowledge the sin

will anyone know there were once silenced voices?
people who swallowed their wisdom
because they lacked hours wasting away on this earth
celestial beings that recognized misbehaving adults
before they took play in part and acted suit

before they no longer knew script versus reality

divorce
unity we once were
laughing and living
together as one
over time,
tiny tears turned to gashing cracks
gashing cracks to gaping holes
my memories race and fight
between idyllic life and peaceful death
mazes we walked
lost in pointless tunnels
fights turning perfect ears forever deaf
no one noticed that by splitting up to find our way out
we named one another 'stranger'
i walk by you now
déjà vu you must be
another life never finished
sweet life or restless death
i see nothing for what it is
we walked away
hoping to find each other
but all I'll ever see of you now
is a ghost
i once called family

separation
it feels weird to be made from two bloods that run like
oil and water
two genes that hate and quarrel
i am the embodiment of failed loved
two worlds that crashed and burned
spoiled and spilled
lost soul meets an angry world

mixed
the colors of your palate spilled
i will forever bear the burden
half in half out
save the dates but no RVSPs
invites,
but no ticket inside
a guessing game of where i'm from
everyone i meet wears a face of confusion
a small glimpse of adoration
a real-life model of future ambition
produce the exotic
fetishize the mystery
ignore the identity
born into a family where no one can relate
two cultures collide
but one person stands alone

close
is a relevant word for you and me
profoundly subjective
inherently contradicting
arrogantly misleading

shattered

people who knew me hurt me
and now i tend to jump to conclusions
i think strangers don't like me
friends must hate me
family never loved me
i don't even give people a chance
those rare coals imprinted their cruelness on me
insecurity is born through those minor interactions
people who knew me hurt me
and now i think those who don't even know me
must despise me
they don't even stand a chance
on my scale of self-doubt

lonely girl
she walks the streets with her head held high
strides of confidence rooted in pain
all who see her earn only a second's glimpse
pain like that can never be spoken
silence might save generations
bury the dead
wear the eulogy on your face
lonely girl walks the street
no one asks her where she's been
no one is waiting for her
she has no destination for she is dead
pretty lonely girl
pretty thing made of glass
and who would want to break such a pretty thing

cradle ages

that gut wrenching feeling that keeps me numb
also reminds me that i'm **alive**

hard ground
would you be quiet?
i don't understand why you're against me
you're making my life unbearable
you're making me uncomfortable
as teammates we clash
false soulmates in this capsuled life
so why do we fight like this?
why can we never get along?
i'm making future plans you can't seem to understand
trust me i know better
you don't understand the pressure
the expectations i live by
acceptance i crave
standards that can't be unset
hers gets along so well
i am jealous of their ease
they listen to each other's wants and needs
i don't care about your needs
make my want your priority
endure the abuse i reign
don't worry
monkey see, monkey do
bully hurts, bully hits
i'm uncomfortable with you
so i critique you with ease
i hate you, leave me be

cradle ages

don't fight my strangle
spare me your caution
head my thoughts and do as i say
if you're a vessel,
i pray i don't break you
but i have slippery hands,
and you're a glass crystal

who let you in?
i never gave you a key
you seep into my life
uninvited
but you don't care
i'm never alone
you're always there
never letting me forget
you're the worst best friend
i could ever hope to have
  - **depression**

perception
i don't care that food is all i think of
if it gives me something to think about
i don't care that i'm hated
if it gives me something to fight against
i don't care to be judged
made a mockery for it all
i don't care because you're mine
i don't care for all the questions
it gives me something to speak of
i don't care for all the judgement
it gives me something to defend
i don't care what you think about me
as long as you're thinking of me

life is better without you
happiness doesn't know you
experience is your friend
peace can't touch you
adventure fears you
you live within me
but i'll always resent you
–anxiety

"control is comfort" said the whisper to the soul
if i eat, will this feeling go away?
if i don't, will it stay?
best way to numb the pain
body bloated by the stress
maybe if i'm smaller,
-my problems might not be easier-
but my solutions will be all the wiser

- **e.d.**

i lost all the weight for nothing
went all the miles to get nowhere
i'm so angry
that i didn't get a chance to enjoy all of my efforts
i want to go back
i miss the way i looked
because i was robbed of my victory meal
and i despise those who stole it

-   **i wasn't ready**

be confident despite never learning how
i'm told daily how to improve my fixed state
how to maculate my current appearance
never knowing what i'm doing
playing catch up while you've mastered the act
how embarrassing for me
effortless to you
and you flaunt this gifted talent
proud of your natural chasms
content that they keep others down
make me feel big
but never in a way a girl would want
towering over and out of place
you fit in the space between
my inner self and crippling reality

words
gossip is toxic,
yet we continue to meddle
lying is fleeting,
yet we continue to fabricate
bullying is abrasive,
yet we continue to gaslight
manipulation is invigorating,
yet we continue to abuse
and all these things are only words

broken
light air
thick sky
happy heart
angry mind
warm body
cold soul
loud voices
lonely nights
for everything i see and hear,
empty is how i always seem to feel

even if you were held accountable
forced to face it all
slammed with every truth
examined every tape
faced with every scene
it probably wouldn't matter
not one ounce
not worth a single breath
see,
i'd rather learn and see my errors
take hold of my mistakes
as long as you do too
i need them held accountable
even if it means me too

to my older sister
i'll never be you
2nd place is the gaping hole i fill by default
i can't escape the comparison
the failure next to your fame
your successor that is never acknowledged
first choice crumbles in my hands
admiration snatched from sight
lost forever because i can't outrun the blood between us
the knot tied for life
men are physical creatures,
and the turning of their heads,
from me to you is all i've known
the beauty you possess
the obsession that follows
i am trampled on the side
a fool trying to run with you
run
run
run
where am i going?
an age i can never beat you to

doorway
i stand on the line of the doorstep
mirrored looks give the illusion that i'm on the inside
yet here I stand
red tape marking my outside bay
lost in the barrier
drowning in the reef

melodies
familiarities
chastity
honesty
-   **this is not what happened**

don't make excuses for them
they are simply not interested
believe me though,
it is their loss
it's not to sound cocky
or delusional of one's own faults
it's just to say that if you're the one confused,
you were probably the most vulnerable
and vulnerable people have a bad habit of moving
mountains and jumping hoops,
for perfectly abled, stiff-necked idiots

what you don't know…
is that you are really living two lives
the one you walk with your own two feet
and the disposable one that hides in me
when you're ready,
i jump, bend, excuse, and live for you
two chances at mortality make you invincible
i'm a lifeless lonely shell
waiting to be turned on by you

bad signs i convince myself have the potential to be good
i know you are terrible for me
a bad influence i see clear as day
i usually care
i usually pivot before my lashes fall
and my wide eyes blink a new opulent stare
but before they even fully close
you and all you embody trap underneath them
stagnant in my mind
imprinted on my heart
this isn't a steady or slow overtaking
you were fast and unapologetic
you steal hours of my thoughts
days of decisions
months of my life
all are wrapped up into you
i can't even help it
Believe me i tried
you were never a good sign
yet the only sign i ever wanted to see

after everything, the least you could do is take some
accountability
don't be petty and blame it on my youth
it never stopped me from being mature
age clearly never stopped you from running back to
little boy games and childish tantrums.
-    **peter pan is an arrogant asshole**

participation winner

problems change their face so often
i never seem to recognize them
i never seem to learn
seeking you out
chasing you down
you're all I know
like a loud wave,
i can't sleep without you near
like battle royale,
we combat
i attack and attack
yet you stand still
powering over me untouched
i come to you with the same control
the same expectations
yet in the relationship of you and i
only one of us remains fearless
only one winner
you may call me the participate

cradle ages

my reasons for discomfort are rarely rational
you burn me once
and i'm forever superstitious of your presence
i only feel happy and full when i'm sad and tearful
I'm only acknowledged at my lowest
and i feel like the happiness i create doesn't belong to me
i'm left with making no sense
fighting futile wars and playing scream matches over pins
that drop on the floor
i'm only content with a plan for improvement in place
a job of perfection in state

i wouldn't be this better version of myself without them
but what hurts is that they'll never know
they can't have the version of me they helped create

i would've stayed small for them
thank goodness they got away

cradle ages

i knew the **ending of our story** before it happened
and yet i lied to myself
because you don't wake yourself up from a good dream
even if you know you're asleep

it's weird.
since then,
every day has been about getting over you
yet,
i feel like you're right here doing it with me

you were special because i made you special
you were sinless because i made you sinless
you were perfect because i made you perfect
my fault for putting you on a pedestal that you constantly
kept trying to jump off of

boxed in
i'm still in the box
yet i'm scared and confused
i'm lost
And i haven't even wandered away
i can't even begin to think outside the box
when i'm too afraid to leave it

copycat
i copy everyone around me
because i don't like what i'm left with when i don't
i'd much rather please you with my agreeance
my opinions shock me
but only because
they originated from someone else's mind
in a perfect world,
i could see things from your perspective
without binding myself to it
i could hear your thoughts
without mirroring them as my own
who even am I?
i'd like to get to know

addict
i'm too tired to step away from tribulations
vices that make my day
try to see it from my side
because i would rather be busy with nothing
than left alone with my own thoughts

2nd row

i see everything from the rearview of your big head
i'm glad you feel everything should be about you
nice to see you resurrect the same problems
just so you stay relevant
egg me on and push me into a corner
just so i'll give you the time of day
what will you do
when your audience gets tired and stops settling for
second place prizes and passive glances?
haven't you heard?
I don't care about your business
you may not have my opinion

i really didn't think we would be one of those awful
stories **i keep hearing about**
i thought everything about us was the impending
explanation of exception over rule
i couldn't comprehend the hypothesis of others proving
true
surely in all the lifetimes lived,
science would fail
the natural course of human emotion would reject the
actions i witnessed emitting out of you
surely,
all the signs would yield faulty
but if the testing of theories has taught me anything
it's that denial is a sure part of the process

cradle ages

how silly of me to think my whole life would begin and end in **one season** of it

i am going to start living my life like it is my own
maybe if i do that enough
surely someday
i'll believe it

-     **thank you for teaching me that making
      one person my whole world is not enough**

cradle ages

it takes thirty seconds of you
for days of healing to go out the window
it takes one call from you
for me to cancel every plan i have
a single look my way
and i forget all direction
- **fully aware but i just can't seem to care**

when it comes to you
you have no idea how many times
i must remind myself
that i don't want to be around anyone
who doesn't want anything to do with me

cradle ages

i'm on the verge of tears
rolling down
rolling down
why can't everything disappear
my legs tapping
body shaking
i'm on the brink
wind pushing me forward
and over

point, no
hello
goodbye
did what we say in between really mean a thing?
did the middle speak for anything?
will our words stand the test of time?
i can tell you hear me not
i know i am too afraid to see
everything i could do for you
all the ways i could share my love
but i am frozen with my words
splitting time and wasting yours
why won't things ever change?
for as long as my promise is easily retractable and my
actions quickly deniable,
i can be as aimless as i feel

aimless
to what avail can i stick to anything
if nothing ever wants to stick back on me?
it takes two to tango in the walk of attachment
a symbiotic relationship i have never seen

the frustrating part
was realizing that you were never going to stop stringing
me along
i had to let go before you would make a choice
because if i stayed
that's all i'd ever be

what i tell myself to get over you
won't fool me anymore
it's numbing and chilling
frustrating and intoxicating
when did i give you this power over me?
how can i get you to leave my mind?
it's shameful how much i factored myself into your life
and you never even thought of mine
why would i care?
how could i want to?
my eyes burn with the memory of what you said
tied to my bed
afraid to function again

you fell first
but i fell harder
when i saw your interest
i encouraged your wonder
i embraced your courage
the same can't be said about you
when you witnessed my reciprocation,
you mounted forth a wall
when you heard my confession,
you ignored my call
you fell first
but I fell harder

barren and deceased
it might be my false hope that broke us
but it was your cheap promises that ended us
vocal symphony of stringless words
lyrical bridges that draw the lie between intention and
fiction

nothing you do ever sees the light of day
because you can't scream lifeless scripts into breathing
moments of existence
save your breaths for the continuing rhythm of the
stories you articulate

beating of your morbid drum
there's a tombstone where your lifeless words lay
stillborn and quiet from your sore mouth
what is more exhausting?
who is more tired?
me or you?
you,
hopelessly stringing expired thoughts
me,
always checking for their resurrection

growing up is realizing that
truth is subjective
but lying is definitive
failure is success
and success is the answer
life never gets easier
phases of it are just simpler
dreams never die
but they can shift
everyone dies
not everyone lives
no one cares about what you make out of your life
more than you

cradle ages

it makes me sad and scared
that I am finally happy without you
that i see hope for my life
even though you're not there
- **i moved on before i thought i would**

sore loser
life just went from hard to harsh
and i don't know why
everything was fine
but now i'm unsure
it was hard to endure
but it's over now
only life won't let me forget
harsh to keep me second guessing
i've made it through
and i'm unable to enjoy it
because anxiety has got me in its grip
and i cannot be content

cradle ages

you were the best distraction
but i knew it was over
when i started needing a distraction from you

it's funny
your emotional instability has imprinted it wildness on
me
like the waves of your mood,
the sensation of missing you comes and goes
the fear of losing you hits hard and fast
and the only thing i can be sure of
is how consistent such inconsistency can be
- **you've become predictable**

cradle ages

i don't believe in soulmates
because if they do exist
that means my soulmate doesn't want me
and i am wiser
than to subject myself to that kind of misery
– **a life i couldn't live**

when did chivalry die?
you took everything that was mine
like loyalty was an art dead and gone
like love was a switch you could turn on and off
fairytales had me put so much faith in who you claimed
to be
but not far off from the castle you started to climb
a lonely steed wanders the woods
because it has no chivalrous knight to call its owner

cradle ages

when you cheated me emotionally
i should have known you would cheat physically

when i had to defend you endlessly
i wish i knew you'd pretend to not know why

despite speaking of you constantly
i now know that with my absence
you also forgot my existence

all the signs were there

it bothers me that it doesn't bother you
it confuses me that it doesn't make you reminisce
what i would give
to live life with your sense of oblivion
   -   **not broken**

cradle ages

i used to pity you for her existence
but now i yell
a million miles away
from my shallowed bone ignorance
hand in hand
the past meets present
they wait for future

-   **your ex**

i try so hard
i forget the difference
between balancing and breathing
checking and wanting
i can't hear you anymore
i walk alone
and i lay down
because it is clear to me
that this depth shall never see a high

i don't live when i'm without you
my life doesn't follow motion
and my days are agony
i must love myself enough to call a spade a spade
i'm too young to wish my days away
simply because you're not in them
simply because
my life is a life yours chose not to see that day

brass painted gold
i'm better alone
ache for realness
chase only fakeness
–complainer

sabotage
my life has always been dictated by the unconscious
plausible thoughts around me
thoughts that often never see the light of day

build a fort
hide for sport
i am tortured for my presence
guilt ridden by my short comings
blurred by bias
saved by chaos
- **invisible**

to be loved by everyone must be nice
but to be your enemy only means
i'm hated by all those who flock around you
whispers and snickers i hear
only add to my sense of inferiority
isolation is my only solution and i like it
because if i can't be comfortable with myself
i don't stand a shot with anyone else

if only
strangers didn't stay a mystery
certain people weren't stuck in history
known for centuries
untouchable for infinity
if only
anything i said had a sense of urgency
a hint of complacency
a note of priority
a sense of sincerity
if beauty grows despite hostility,
why is it ignored with such tenacity?
why does a world deprived of such a necessity,
find joy in its obstinance?
sport in its extremity?
regressing literally
fighting it obviously
hoping against it honestly
critically, insistently, and earnestly halting its state of
exigency

it's not that deep
but it is to me
it's not that deep
yet it floods my thoughts
it's not that deep
yet i am drowning in this play-pin pool
it's not that deep
yet i forgot how to swim
it's not that deep
yet i'm sinking in
choking on water
grasping for air
it's not that deep
yet I can't see the surface
you are standing next to me fine and unbothered
yet i am in deep
it's not that deep
but all i see is everything i can lose
"it's not that deep" said the girl in too deep
she's just not standing on her own two feet

too much and you hate it
not enough and you crave it
to have it is to feel heard
to not is to feel pointless
to lose it hurts more than never having it
to gain it feels like one has done right
to earn it is to have pride for someone else
to work for it means its conditional
to give it is an investment
to pretend you have it is exhausting
to steal it is to be full of it
to share it is to know it's worth
to learn it for yourself is the best thing you'll ever do
to throw it away is either wise or careless
either way
at the end of the day
there never seems to be enough to go around
–attention

chess is a game i like to play with you
misdirection and poker glances
i forgot that face to face
we are yet opponents still
with simple words
you attack from left field
but little do you know
my percentile matches your wit
winners can't suffer from far sighted vision
my acting face cold and safe
playing dumb for the sake of genius charm
lookout
your queen meets my rook
game on

the sun sets before the problem is solved
before the tears dry
and the salty air grows stale
shouldn't i enjoy this unanticipated happiness?
or should we wait to reconcile before anger muddles our
words?
i don't want to hear the intention behind your actions
when they are still met with repetition
for now,
they are only excuses

love's antonym
you thought we were soulmates
i was unaffected
putting on a show
playing dress up
doing what you needed
saying what you wanted
i used to think i didn't know love
but the truth is,
you never really showed it to me
you talked
i listened
you asked
i acted
i invested
you accepted
this is not love
not the kind i want

i've run many marathons
without ever leaving the foot of my bed
i've lived through many interactions
without ever moving my lips
i've witnessed many scenarios
without ever having to be surrounded by company
the things my mind can create
the possibilities it formulates
leave me too tired to get up
and desire the **reality at hand**

cradle ages

the battle in my mind
is **whether or not** to be mean enough
that you can't move on
or nice enough
that you feel like you can reach back out

being a girl
stumbling between saying too much
and never leading you on
struggling with remaining a mystery
but also easily approachable
balancing effortless looks and timeless beauty
one of the guys
but also so much more
accomplished
but not overpowering
smart
but not too intimidating
living in the space between your capabilities
and the standards you expect
skinny
but has an appetite
pretty
but only naturally
constant effort to be ready whenever you call
not expecting too much
but also never knowing what i deserve
overthinking every subliminal message?
sure
but then again
i've been programmed to think my entire existence
runs on the timetable of your interest
haunted by casualness

cradle ages

yet chasing the title of one in a million
not too easy
but never a prude
constant thinking
but forever belittled
smart
but not smarter
funny
but not as funny
rich
but not richer
busy
but always free
accomplished
but not nearly more accomplished
than you will ever be

waiting can be so painful
that false promises are the only way i can cope
but i spend so much time preparing for a false
hypothetical future
i am often not ready for the reality that comes

cradle ages

for a mere second
i saw it all
a reason better than being the greatest
a purpose larger than my fakeness
an experience worth my energy
if i could see the things you tell me,
then maybe i could stop obsessing
over all the little things i can't seem to let go
–rationality

sleep pills
my imagination used to help me fall asleep
now it just makes me sad
for what i witness behind my eyes
is never evident in my real world
what a life i live when i go to sleep
everything i'm afraid to do,
i choose
who i want to be,
i am
all the things i want,
i have
obstacles solved
relationships fixed
will any of the self-harbored melatonin i create in my
head,
ever breathe existence into my reality?

speaking from nothing
i tried to wait it out
cite my sources
back my opinion
but no chance ever came
opportunity didn't strike
life never unfolded
so here i am
take what you shall
unbridled,
unaltered,
celibate opinions

sexism
you sit very righteously
quite willful and proud on one's throne of accomplice
you invalidate my reasons as excuses
maybe they are
but don't lecture me on willpower
when i'm pulling a cargo ship
and you're strolling right through the door
carpet rolled out and your front seat saved
i'm on the waitlist
but your road is already paved

individual
if i detach from you
who will i be?
i am scared
i barely like myself as it is

introvert
i'm starting to think i enjoy my own company way too
much
i can't be bothered by other people anymore
i'm a lifeless shell
too exhausted to lift a finger of compassion
want nothing
give nothing
i'm starting to think the healthiest thing for me to do
is to start hating myself a little more
this type of isolation can only brood resentment

it wasn't hope i was keeping alive
it was impending disappointment

it's harder to accept the things
we have the ability to control
- **toxic cycle**

ruler
i like to measure myself
against everything i'll never be
and nothing i want out of this life

cradle ages

i don't fear **death**
i fear the loneliness that comes with it

thief
a cruel joke time has on me
it has robbed me of you
it's made sure our paths never cross
time is selfish
because i will only ever have the thought of you

emotionally battered people
often lose their footing and fear interaction
avoidance is a god send
and silence is never found
don't put them in charge
they squirm at making choices
to busy calculating morphed feelings of impossible beings

maze
strangers who stay hidden
puzzles that remain scattered
paradigms keep me lost
chasms that trap me in
abyss with no floor
that is the wonder of you

you don't exist

maybe i'm just unlucky in love

wished upon that star so hard it broke

tossed that coin so hard it sunk

maybe some dreams never break from the nights grasp

but all i'm asking for is what i was told every girl gets

i was promised a chance

but i guess i got the time wrong

because it never came

face and face and face pass me by

can i afford my expectations?

will anyone even ask me my standards?

will any conversation last longer than an introduction?

does any boy know that a smile is all i crave?

bare minimum girls get so much hate

but at least they don't have to wait

mortal life, infinite love
where and when?
sometimes i think soulmates have expiration dates
i missed to many chances
turned down too many yes's
i feel like i've grown stagnant to the idea of love
numb toward its touch
deaf to its sound
sometimes i fear that my soulmate never existed
what if they left this earth a long time ago?
dead and gone
never to be known
would i have felt their death?
cheated of their life
our life
robbed of my grief
who am i to them?
how many times have i crossed them in the street?
their face striking me cordless
blind to the future held between us
where have i walked that your feet also touched?
what air have we shared?
what stories do we know?
what words have we used?
who am i to you?
a ghost, a dream, a future, a past, a second
i pray every day that my mortal life didn't ruin my
infinite love

every language i can't speak is a beautiful one
every conversation i don't hear is a kind one
every action whose intention i didn't know was a noble
one
every smile i see is an innocent one
every lesson i haven't learned is a good one
but the language i speak is poor
every conversation i have is bad
every action i take is small
every smile i make is guilty
every lesson i learn hurts
i am the **black sheep** of the world

stare at you long enough and i might recognize who's
looking back at me
analyze every muscle and expression
every wrinkle and line
stare at you long enough
and everything i see will surely blur
the story i tell myself
and the reality you lived
stare at you long enough
and i might have some empathy
stare at you long enough
and i might gain some sympathy
the days that catapulted you here
inertia pushes the past forward
it pushes you to me
in my face
and i can't ignore you staring me down
i don't recognize the pain that changed you
iris to iris
you are the same to me
but your smile looks forced
and your eyes look tired
stare at you long enough
and i might not question what brought you here to me
-    **what i see in the mirror**

part two

dedicated to those grounding revelations that often
moralize life itself and the humanity that succumbs to it

to my self-worth,
i'm sorry
but i'm learning
the world handed me a ruler
but i now follow a new measuring system
and the two cannot convert

cradle ages

dreams
a desired possibility
not a required reality

you were once in me
now you surround me
fleeting and running
you are no use to me now
others need you more
i'll be here
breathing in someone new

- **air**

prisoner
what people don't tell you
is that embracing what does not come naturally
also means enduring life
when you feel it is not your own

pros vs. cons
i know you feel like i needed you
maybe i did
maybe i do
but i'm much better off this way
because who walks around on crutches
with no broken leg?

opinions are birthed through personal life
that is why in the midst of disagreement
people take such deep offense

it doesn't help that some people
can be so harsh in their delivery

people treating you like shit doesn't bother you
because everyone has a hierarchy of priority
and attention simply means so much more
-   **priorities**

hopeless romantic
with a dirty mind
-   **endurance**

i fear **satisfaction** with every fiber of my being
what will i crave?
will my bones race faster toward death's cold touch,
if i settle for less than what i fought for?
will my heart break from the tragedy?
my dreams will never forgive me for abandoning them
when they carried me through many sleepless nights
my soul will never know
what celestial aspiration was its destiny
where to stop?
where to begin?
i grow tired at the thought
of everything losing meaning and point
every hope finding its destination
every question finding its answer
every story finding its conclusion

cradle ages

i'm not embarrassed to be **vulnerable**
one day,
real people will appreciate it

if anything,
your pathetic approach to avoiding accountability makes
me laugh
i won't let your toxic mindset that the right one will
change you,
ignite a sense of inferiority within me
your behavior is rooted deep within you
tangled far down within your soul
and no perfect person can or should
go through those deep trenches of your dark underbelly
to do the dirty work of pulling out your mangled weeds
of affluent arrogance

- **no one else's problem but your own**

i don't want to know what you're doing anymore
i fully believe nothing my mind extravagantly illustrates
will make up for your **shallow presence**

independence isn't a choice we make once and leave be
independence is a state we must guard and protect with
all our heart
we cannot frolic between assurance of its presence
and our absence with its intention
in our actions
in our words
in our choices
everything and everyone can compromise our
independence
when we abandon our sense of self
we lose our independent zest for life

i don't miss **childhood** at all
but i do miss feeling like a child
so much
i miss the simplicity of it
i often find myself fighting time itself
trying to go back to it
keeping my nails and hair short
wearing clothes longer than i should
comfort is wholeheartedly found in the days
i feel wrapped in childlike wonder
anything to go back to that simpler time in my life
the comfort i felt knowing i was only a kid
and nothing could really hurt me

i've decided that i know nothing
i will continue to get it wrong
and i will never be completely satisfied
i have never felt such freedom

what you need in life is not a reflection of fact
but rather a measure
of how much you are willing to let it affect you

i knew more than i ever let on
i played dumb
because i am wiser than to deny the part of the fool
even after everything,
i still bite my tongue on things you'll never know
sometimes i feel like i might burst under the weight of
my secrecy
but then i remember,
i am happy to give you the gift of ignorance
and the overwhelming paranoia you have to live with

right now i just feel stupid
embarrassed for being bewildered, humbled, and silenced
by your harsh cutthroat analysis of you and i
right now i wish i had snapped
for every nasty threat you lashed,
i wanted to yell back twice as hard
but i am a loving person
and for everything you took from me
you may not have my goodness

me, myself, and i take a new form in my life away from
you
and i like it
i really like it
i love it

cradle ages

fresh ideas...
rooted in lessons
limited by access
born from mistakes
created out of knowledge
mastered through experience
-   **maturity**

the joy in my life is a collection
of every good thing i never expected
and every bad thing
that is bound to someday make me laugh

i want something for myself
as willpower dies within me
but i want something for myself
even though sacrifice hurts me greatly
yet i want something for myself
and though it's costly
still,
i want something for myself
i won't know if it's worth it until i have it
surely,
if i give in now
i'll always wonder
did that something want me too?

what i need
is exactly what finds me
what doesn't come
was never meant for me
what comes my way
is always in perfect time
what i attract
is what was made for me
    -   **law of attraction**

acceptance
you don't have to be exactly where you want to be
in order to love yourself
endure life and embrace what does not come naturally

regulate

when i am hurt,

i sabotage recovery

by envisioning in my mind what healing looks like

and how it will happen

when i am scared,

i often overindulge future events

to match the anxiety i am feeling in the present

when i am sad,

i am better left alone

until i feel like my own life

is an out of body experience

cradle ages

to those who love us
there is no distinction between the light in our life
and the darkness in it
so,
keep my love fresh in your mind
so that it is evident in your times of stress

ignorance is bliss
last night i had a wonderful thought
a riveting realization
but i fell asleep before i could write it down
and now i can't remember anything at all
now all i hold is the memory of its presence
without the knowledge of its content
i took for granted my inability to hold captive every
thought
it's like they were never my own
ran away from the grasp of their creator
who knows where this notion ran to?
or where this aspiration lost conception?
i wish i could retain my memory
but it's gone now
gone for good
it's futile to fight it
unwanted ignorance still broods bliss
sometimes life hands you what you didn't know you
needed

cradle ages

do you ever look back at a time in your life
and forget that you once lived through it?
sometimes i look back on days
and tailored emotions fill me
acquitted and associated
bias and favored
good days and bad days
they vary on the spectrum of tolerance
but all untouchable now
all locked away from alteration
no matter the depth of their gravity
they will all forever be
only simple memories

-growth

my life begins when my fear of you ends
our paths will cross
it's only a matter of time
but going forward
i will welcome you old friend
like the wise owl you are
because your sting is quick,
your push only so hard,
and your bite only so deep

    -   **failure**

i refuse to do anything that requires me to abandon
myself
i love **her**
she is my fortress of strength
i will not chase other souls
over the one who's always walked with me
i care for her peace too much to be the one that robs it
she has earned her rest
for her
i will learn loyalty
i will learn respect
she has my whole heart
i will not abandon her

my **stillness** comes from a good place
my stillness is a result of my observations
motion causes change
and life is good
life is still
i am happy here with myself
i wouldn't change a thing

cradle ages

when you hit a **red light**
don't get scared
when you reach a crossroads
don't panic
inhale
exhale
ride deep breaths
like honeycomb rides through a honey jar
evaluate your options
consider your choices
and remember
never fear the unknown of what life might hold
because with most things,
embracing comes before enjoying

reaping the outcomes
of my consequential mistakes
putting in the work
doing my time
taking grace where i can find it
giving love despite losing it

    - **warrior**

cradle ages

i used to think the loudest people made the most impact
i felt guilty for not possessing the trait
of longevity in my lungs
had their way time and time again
but **silence** is my friend
she has served me well
she has taught me resilience
she has saved me in times i wouldn't know until the
dawn set for the next
she has showed me perseverance
she has moved me from small tables with ignorant people
to big rooms with loving stewards
i used to think being quiet meant i was always alone
but the breath of silence was the company of my future
pulling me out of those moments
catapulting me to better people
if i spoke too soon,
others might have tried to steal my good thing to come
hold on to good things

i am **content**
for i have one life
and i would rather live happily
and realize after that i wasted it
than know i'm wasting it every day
by refusing to be happy

cradle ages

i'm afraid of you
because i don't know you
what are you capable of?
too many wonders i could never fathom
who are you?
a friend of mine?
surely one can hope
- **peace**

what is life
if not to feel every emotion,
and then chase your favorites
all over again

everything is a law of attraction
so radiate goodness and give love freely
you'll find it in return
but remember,
everything is a law of attraction
so if you're going to be a positive person,
watch out for those negative drainers
- **bad magnets**

my mantras

1. if i'm not pursing my passion, then i'm actively pursuing my fear

2. i am thankful i had the realization, so i'm grateful i get to do the work

3. the biggest obstacle to overcome is myself

4. it's going to be great because i've already decided it will be

5. everything is only an adventure, so in the end, it can't really hurt me

6. die by oneself and that's where i'll find true perseverance

7. doing something hard hurts, but not doing it may prove to be much harder later

aging makes me wiser
tougher, thicker skin
temperament controlled
peace of mind instilled
comforts established
conditions practiced
serenity of life is found
in my steady rhythm

if you only look straight,
all you will see
is your future-self pulling you forward

- **dreamers**

time
i hate minutes
i am forever bound to their will
they're slow when i want them to be long
they're fast when i want them to be slow
seconds are too tedious
hours are too big
so,
i'm left with minutes
forever fighting their power with rage

brown eyes
blue eyes
green eyes
for all the color in this world
remember most life is
lived in the gray
- **few things are black and white**

dance **when** the music plays
cry when the movie ends
laugh when the joke is told
speak when the silence is loud
sleep when the moon wakes
breathe when the problem overflows
listen when the one you love talks
hug when the greetings end
smile when the life you have is good

warmth in picture perfect form
i want to look onto the day ahead
as though its full of daisies
flowers warming the gaze ahead
sunny glows lighting my path
feeling heard through walking away
from competition i didn't need
shows i didn't wish to attend
and people i no longer want

crush

oh my goodness
i just saw a real-life walking definition of pretty
you
drop dead gorgeous
please don't take my stone-cold face
for automatic disdain
your beauty humbled me fast
your eyes stole my words
your disposition makes me mad
choking on my thoughts
so they never stand a chance
seeing the light of day
you need a warning label
because everything about you is unfair
flashing that witty smile
i just melt
like a concrete setting backwards
mold me as you may
because you're so pretty
i can't help but look away
please approach
don't let me fool you
shy smiles simply show my fear of rejection
so I'm putting on my face of solitude
wielded self-protection

happy wall
make a list of all the things that make you happy
and tape it to your heart
make it tall and strong
like a wall of positivity
to fight off the bad days yet to come

a cup of coffee
makes me warm
keeps me sharp and witty
but just like you
too much a good thing
and i am good for nothing

flowers **all the time**
dropping honey on my spine
hold everything
close to mind
heart and hand
together all the time
sweetness in mind

average joe
i am not special in the way i thought i'd be
no drop dead looks
never stopped in the streets
no perfect body
no fame or bane for leadership
i'm not popular or well-versed
i do not live an outstanding or exotic life
i am average
but despite these things
i am indeed special
there's no one else on this earth that could ever be me
my DNA lives within me and me alone
the generations that made me cannot be copied
a replica cannot be produced
only new to come
future lives yet to breathe
as hard as it is at times to walk in my shoes
no one else has
no one else ever will
these are my shoes
they are mine
i am not special
i am more than that
i am rare

a caterpillar goes its whole life never knowing what it
will be
even as it builds its cocoon
it doesn't know of what's to come
instinct is not understanding
who knows what steps i'm taking today
will play a part in who i will be
-    **faith**

mystery
when you look at me
i hope i don't give it all away
i hope i keep the mystery alive
i'd love to know where your mind's eye first runs to
when you see me
what did your imagination create?
listening to your train of thought when my finger trickles
down your spine

i'm happy to not be right
if it means you get to be
it doesn't matter
when you smile
curtains of age unveil
shining pupils of youth
the rest of the world goes quiet
reason holds no stalk
all i see is you
-     **true beauty**

don't worry
one day,
you will understand it
one day,
you will master what you can't even begin to
comprehend
if anything,
let that give you peace
- **learning**

cradle ages

to find simplicity in life,
you must chase it

and to chase it
means running away
from everything that ruins it

happiness isn't coming
i must go out and find it
from this
to that
through you
for me

steps

if i was taller,
i could take bigger steps
but i'm not
i can only put one foot so far in front of the other
when i was younger and shorter
a few steps took a lifetime
now a million goes by fast
i used to wish i could take bigger steps
i hate seeing the path ahead
without being able to move there
but if i could take bigger steps,
i might miss the million little things
that make each step special
in its own perfect way

half full

today i got up
and everything made me smile
it didn't come naturally
forced inoculation
but once i started,
it felt too good to stop
once I tried it,
i couldn't remember life without it

when life is good and you know it
take a mental picture
it costs nothing
but is worth everything
   -   **a good deal**

deep ocean
drowning or resting?
seeking or hidden?
protected by the waves of your will
or crushed by their impact?
for my soul is indefinite in the face of destruction
for my flesh is of this world
and it cannot fully know you
let it be crushed by the ocean,
darkened by space
surrendered to the enemy
because my soul can never be lost

soothe
my eyes burn
sleep won't do the trick
it's you they need
brush your finger across my lashes
and soothe my teary eyes
cradle them back to sleep

cradle ages

i dream of you always
your imaginative love warms me from the inside
and i become soup in your arms
i wake up and you're gone
but does it mean more
that you chose to search my inside first?
you sunk in past my wall of perfection
and like the trojan horse
you took capture of me
without me even knowing your entrance
falling hard
i'm not ready to greet the world
i want to sleep so i can be with you
always and forever

a growing flower
when you grow
you must ripen
stripped of browned petals
freed from dead leaves
don't fear the growing of your stem
the ground is where your problems lay
the soil is your past
those things have hurt you
let them go
let them help you grow
look to the sky
it's where you're headed
it's where your future awaits

finding feminity
1. be gentle
2. be confident in who you are
3. eat with passion
4. stay driven toward your goals
5. deep breaths
6. don't live in the context of time
7. romanticize your life
8. self-care always

something so scary and sweet about starting over
i used to dread the idea of sharing every intimate part of
myself all over again
i used to fear the rejection that almost always came
when did I give my ability to self-love over to nameless
strangers?
i am not a battery that is charged by the outlet of others
i radiate what is buried within my very bones
encoded in my very being
welded to my simple soul
i radiate the **miracoulousness of my existence**

cradle ages

being loved by you
goes against every definition
of love i have ever been told

for that i thank you
because i didn't like the **idea of love**
until i met you

dependent

energy is what the sun is to the world
watcher is what the sky is to the land
giver is what the mother is to the child
family is what the day is to the night
brother is what the ocean is to the sea
reliever is what the warmth is to the cold
hope is what the tree is to the bird
friend is what the bee is to the flower
neighbor is what the stars are to the planet
lover is what you are to me

i love you
that's all i want to say
too many words muddle intensity
rob me of depth and meaning
don't analyze my every move
trust each action as it flows
from my heart to yours
i love you
simply and purely

when you don't know what to do,
do nothing
- **my greatest life lesson**

i have so much love in my heart
i don't know where to put it
i wish i could just lock it up
save it for a rainy day
but since i can't
i'll just leave it here
out in the open
free for the taking
use as needed
- **free money**

your voice is like soft silk to warm skin
hot soup for a heavy sinus
sweet honey for a dry throat
warm blanket on a cold night
sweet colors on a dreary day
light rain on a lonely windowpane

cradle ages

in those times
of true golden nuggets of joy
i know you helped plant the seed
i know you helped me grow
-   **you're my water**

soulmates
there's an invisible line
connecting me to you
rearranging my insides
pumping me with dopamine
there's something in your eyes
that can only talk to mine
i don't fear silence between us
it reminds me of a summer day
a warm hug
a moment's peace
never two strangers more intertwined
than you and i
talk and time is never cheap
but you'd spend a fortune on me

end of the world
there is so much in this world
too much for there to be any means for me
but that's okay
because i fit right here
next to you
and i'm okay removing the pressure
of having to be anything
do anything
accomplish much
because if it all ended tomorrow,
i would be okay
nothing gets better than the ease of you

synergy
like an imaginative friend,
he was always right here
she spoke her mind
and like clockwork
his voice whispered deep within her
overtime,
his voice and hers meshed to one
and suddenly
all aspects of her personality had changed

pretty things and ugly places
one can make the other
but also destroy it
the first can save the latter
but also succumb to it

greetings
good morning my baby
good luck my precious
goodbye my forever
good afternoon my darling
good day my honey
good evening my love
goodnight my sweetheart

the consequence of always being with you
means never knowing happiness without you
a risk i'm willing to take
- **gambler**

i have found that i feel the **strongest**
when i am gentle with myself
gentle with my words
gentle with my thoughts
gentle with my intentions
gentle with my actions
and gentle with my heart
this is when i am my best
it is always when i am trying the least

if the future has you
then i know everything was worth it
every wrong decision was the right step
every painful encounter was a needed lesson
someday i will be forever grateful
for anything and everything
that brought me here to you

sometimes i wish something **catastrophic** would
happen
just so i could have a reason
to call that catastrophic being
and have them walk right back into my life

but then i remember
all the joy
all the realizations
and all the happiness
that came once that catastrophic being left

i remember everything i did because of them
everything i did in spite of them
so now
instead of going backwards
i'm going to try living with a new philosophy
i'm going to lookout for the next catastrophe coming
and dive headfirst
knowing it's better to go through it and see the
rainbow
than it is to drown under its control

my hero
you've waited so long for your time to come
i've waited years
you've waited centuries
still the patience eats at me
and you stay still and strong
how can i compare to your purity?
yet alone you stand
i am ash
and you are everything
in one breath you spoke the earth into order
yet i have fallen out of place
how do i know which way to go?
this race in which i haven't made up my mind
help me see that you are here and king
i have no need to run

i like to think
that every line in your hand
every crease of your palm
is a story and a road
of how you found your way home to me
- **why our hands fit so perfectly**

accomplish something bigger than yourself
and that will give you confidence
- **bigger picture**

to my childhood enemy,
i age
fall through time and space
more of my life is lived floating out of body
fragments of my childhood are like
sharp glass hidden as blades of grass
more often than i hope
i am back there
more often than i want
you are still right here
in my face
attacking my life, body, and soul
more often than i should be
i am still that little kid
hopeless and helpless
more often than not
i don't seem to move on
swallowed by hurdles that catapult others
minutes to hours
pen to paper
and this i now know
tomorrow will come
this vision of my past will fade
this low will become a high
i will escape this
i've already decided it
for every more often,
there is a most often

most often i am changed
most often i am loved
most often i am healing
most often i am free of you

cradle ages

thank you

Printed in Great Britain
by Amazon